CW00919091

Office of Government Commerce   London:TSO

First edition Crown copyright 1997
Second edition 2002
Third edition 2005
Sixth Impression 2007

ISBN 0 11 330979 1 (Sold in a pack of 10 copies)
ISBN 0 11 330985 6 (Single copy ISBN)

For further information regarding this and other OGC products please
contact:

OGC Service Desk
Rosebery Court
St Andrews Business Park
Norwich
NR7 0HS
Telephone: +44 (0) 845 000 4999

e-mail: ServiceDesk@ogc.gsi.gov.uk

Website: www.ogc.gov.uk

Printed in the United Kingdom for The Stationery Office
N5561595   04/07   19585   321859

CONTENTS

INTRODUCTION

Most organisations are experiencing unprecedented levels of change. Change has become a way of life for organisations that need to remain effective and competitive in order to thrive. It is essential to manage the inherent risk associated with change and innovation.

Projects bring together resources, skills, technology and ideas to deliver business benefits or to achieve business objectives. Good project management helps to ensure that these benefits or objectives are achieved within budget, within time and to the required quality.

PRINCE2 is a project management method designed to provide a framework covering the wide variety of disciplines and activities required within a project. The focus throughout PRINCE2 is on the Business Case, which describes the rationale and business justification for the project. The Business Case drives all the project management processes, from initial project set-up through to the finish of the project.

The complete description of PRINCE2 can be found in *Managing Successful Projects with PRINCE2*, published by The Stationery Office. This Pocketbook is produced as an aide-memoire and handy reference for project personnel who are familiar with the method and its terminology.

CONCEPTS

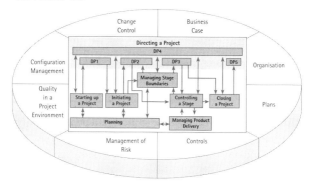

PRINCE2 is a project management method for all types of project. PRINCE2 focuses on the management aspects, such as the Business Case, project organisation, plans, controls, quality and risk, and separates these from the specialist task of delivering the outputs of the project (which may include procured products).

PRINCE2 is 'process-based' in that all the project management activities may be easily scaled up or down to suit the requirements of the project.

Throughout the project, PRINCE2 encourages the Project Manager and Project Board to focus on the business justification of the project. At the end of each stage, the Business Case is reviewed to ensure continued viability of the project.

4

PRINCE2 encourages and supports involvement of the user(s) and all the other stakeholders who have an interest in the project's outcome or who are affected by it in any way.

A PRINCE2 project is sub-divided into stages to provide assessment points for senior management to monitor progress and control the project. The end of a stage represents a key decision and commitment point.
The number of stages is totally flexible, based on such considerations as project size, complexity, risk, significance and criticality.

If the project is part of a programme, PRINCE2 provides the necessary interfaces with programme management.

PRINCE2 is designed to meet requirements of recognised quality management standards.

Customer/supplier relationship

PRINCE2 assumes that within any project there are various groups of people with specific interests in the project and its outcome, including:

- Customers who have commissioned the work and will be benefiting from the end results
- Users who will use or operate the final product(s) (the customer and user may be the same group of people in some situations)

- Suppliers who are providing specialist resources and/or skills to the project, or are providing goods and services.

PRINCE2 recognises that the customer and supplier may come from separately managed areas and typically from commercially separate organisations.

Tailoring

PRINCE2's concepts and processes represent good management practices in project management. Each concept and process needs to be applied to suit the specific needs of the project. Tailoring the method involves consideration of such issues as project size, risk, cost, duration, quality, importance and location. Tailoring to suit the circumstances is critical to the successful application of PRINCE2. The philosophy behind each concept and process in PRINCE2 can be applied to both the smallest and the largest projects.

PROJECT MANAGEMENT PROCESSES

PRINCE2 has eight management processes, each providing a particular emphasis throughout the project life cycle. Any project run under PRINCE2 will address each of these processes in some form. The processes are not sequential, step-by step, through the project; some can be done in parallel with others. The key to successful use of PRINCE2 is to ask: 'How extensively should this process be applied on this project?' for each of the eight processes.

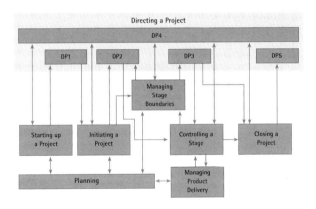

Directing a Project (DP)

This process runs from start-up through to closure of the project and is aimed at the management level above the Project Manager, namely the Project Board. This process defines the Project Board's responsibilities for:

- Approving the Project Brief and authorising initiation
- Authorising the Project Initiation Document, including the Business Case, and taking 'ownership' of the project
- Checking project status at the end of each stage before authorising continuation to the next stage
- Providing management direction and guidance to the Project Manager, and reacting to exception situations
- Liaising with corporate or programme management
- Confirming project closure.

Starting up a Project (SU)

This is a pre-project process, designed to answer the basic question: 'Do we have a viable and worthwhile project?' This process will:

- Ensure the necessary authority exists for undertaking the project
- Ensure that sufficient information is available about the project's objectives, scope and constraints
- Design and appoint an appropriate project management team
- Decide on the approach to be used to deliver the required outputs from the project
- Create the initiation Stage Plan.

Initiating a Project (IP)

This is the project process that ensures that the project can be successfully scoped and managed to its completion by laying down a firm foundation. This process will:

- Ensure that everyone involved understands the scope and objectives of the project
- Ensure that a suitable Business Case exists for the project
- Ensure that the project has been adequately planned and costed
- Assess the risks identified
- Obtain the commitment from the Project Board to proceed to the next stage.

Initiation should be the first stage of any project.

Controlling a Stage (CS)

This process covers the day-to-day management activities on the project. Throughout a stage, this will consist of a cycle of:

- Authorising work to be done by the project team
- Monitoring and reporting progress
- Capturing Project Issues
- Assessing required changes
- Taking necessary corrective action
- Taking delivery of completed products from the project team.

Managing Product Delivery (MP)

This process separates the management of the project from the creation or provision of products by the project team. It involves:

- Negotiating and accepting Work Packages from the Project Manager
- Ensuring the required work is done

- Reporting on progress
- Ensuring completed products meet required quality criteria
- Obtaining approval for completed products.

Managing Stage Boundaries (SB)

This process covers the Project Manager's responsibilities at the end of each stage, or, if the project is in exception, enables a corrective plan to be put forward. It involves:
- Reporting on delivery of products
- Reassessing the risk situation
- Updating project management documentation
- Planning the next stage, or producing an Exception Plan.

Closing a Project (CP)

This process ensures a clear end to the project, whether it is successful completion or early termination, by:
- Reporting on fulfilment of project objectives defined in the Project Initiation Document
- Recommending required follow-on actions
- Planning post-project review(s)
- Assessing the way the project was managed and reporting lessons learned
- Decommissioning the project.

Planning (PL)

This process describes the iterative steps involved in planning and replanning the project. It is used during the activities of the other PRINCE2 processes. Planning in PRINCE2 uses the product-based planning technique to ensure plans are based on required products:

- Write a Product Description for the final product
- Create a Product Breakdown Structure which identifies the products required
- Write Product Descriptions, which include defining the quality requirements, for each product
- Draw a Product Flow Diagram to show the logical order of creation of the products and their interdependencies
- Identify activities required to create the products
- Estimate duration and effort for each activity
- Assess the risks
- Calculate the costs
- Identify management control points needed
- Document the plan, its assumptions and supporting text.

COMPONENTS

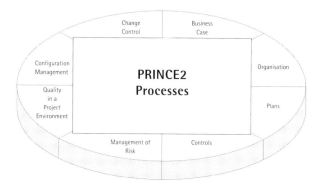

There are a number of key aspects of project management that are used throughout the PRINCE2 processes.

Business Case
A PRINCE2 project is 'driven' by its Business Case, which defines the justification and rationale for the project, including the benefits expected and an assessment of costs against these benefits.

The Business Case must embrace all the elements that are affected by the project, not just the most significant element. For example, avoid focussing the Business Case (and hence the project) on the benefits of new equipment whilst ignoring the impact on personnel, accommodation and changed working practices.

The Business Case is 'owned' by the Executive, who is ultimately responsible for the delivery of benefits from the outcome of the project.

Organisation

However small or large the project, there must be agreement on:

- Who says what is needed
- Who provides the budget
- Who provides the resources
- Who authorises changes
- Who manages the day-to-day work
- Who defines the standards to be met.

On a small project, many of the above will be the responsibility of the same person. On a large project, a number of people may be involved in each of the above. PRINCE2 provides a flexible project management structure consisting of specific roles. Most of these roles may be allocated to one person or shared between a number of people, or combined together.

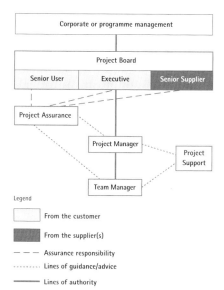

Legend

☐ From the customer

■ From the supplier(s)

— — Assurance responsibility

········ Lines of guidance/advice

——— Lines of authority

Project Board

The Project Board represents the interests of the business
(customer), user and supplier, and provides overall
direction and management of the project. The Project
Board has responsibility and authority for the project
within its remit (the Project Mandate) set by corporate
or programme management. The Project Board is also
responsible for assurance that the project remains on
course to deliver the desired outcome, as defined in the
Business Case.

At the start of a project, the Project Board:
• Approves the Project Brief to commence start-up

- Agrees the Project Manager's responsibilities and objectives
- Decides how Project Assurance is to be carried out
- Commits to resources required for the initiation stage
- Confirms project tolerances
- Approves the Project Initiation Document.

As the project progresses, the Project Board:
- Gives direction and guidance to the Project Manager
- Reviews the project status at the end of each stage and approves progress to the next stage
- Checks the project is still on track to achieve the Business Case
- Reviews and approves any Exception Plans
- Approves changes
- Reports to programme or corporate management
- May recommend project termination.

At the end of the project, the Project Board:
- Checks that all products have been delivered satisfactorily
- Confirms that operational and support groups are prepared to take responsibility for the project's outcome
- Approves the End Project Report, the Lessons Learned Report and the Post-Project Review Plan
- Authorises project closure.

The Project Board consists of three roles: Executive, Senior User and Senior Supplier. These represent the three interests in a project: business, user and supplier. PRINCE2 is flexible in how many people are required to cover these interests. Roles can be combined or shared according to the project needs. Project Board members must have the capability to make decisions and commit the resources required.

Executive

The Executive is the individual with ultimate accountability for the success of the project. The Executive has to ensure that the project represents value for money and follows a cost-conscious approach whilst balancing the needs of the business, users and suppliers. The Executive 'owns' the project's Business Case.

Senior User

The Senior User role is accountable for ensuring that requirements are fully and accurately specified, making sure that what is delivered is fit for purpose and that the solution meets users' needs within the constraints of the Business Case.

Senior Supplier

This role represents the resources providing design, development, facilitation, procurement and implementation of the project's products.

Project Manager

The Project Manager has the authority to run the project on a day-to-day basis on behalf of the Project Board. The prime responsibility is to ensure that the project delivers the required products to the required standard of quality and within the specified constraints of time and cost.

During the project, the Project Manager will:
- Prepare project documentation, including Project Initiation Document, Project and Stage Plans
- Obtain Project Board approval of all plans
- Define responsibilities and allocate work within the project
- Monitor and control progress within tolerance levels agreed with the Project Board
- Manage the risks, including development of any required contingency plans
- Negotiate the performance and delivery of Work Packages with the Team Manager(s)
- Schedule stage control points
- Liaise with Project Assurance
- Prepare and present reports for the Project Board, for example, at the end of each stage
- Enforce quality and change control procedures
- Ensure Risk, Quality and Issue Logs are maintained and used effectively
- Prepare any Exception Plans should tolerance levels be threatened.

Team Manager

This is an optional role, likely to be required on larger projects where teams of different skills are needed. The role may also be relevant where the work of the project is being done by a third party reporting to the customer's Project Manager.

The Team Manager will:
- Negotiate Work Packages with the Project Manager
- Plan and allocate work within the team
- Monitor team progress and initiate any required corrective action
- Report progress and issues to the Project Manager
- Maintain details of quality checks carried out
- Liaise with Project Assurance.

Project Assurance

Project Assurance provides the check that the project continues to meet its specification, the required standards and the Business Case. Project Assurance is the responsibility of each Project Board member; however, the role can be delegated but it must be independent of the Project Manager. Each of the following aspects of Project Assurance should be covered:

Business:
- Focus on the Business Case is maintained
- Risks are being controlled
- Liaison is maintained between customer and supplier
- Expenditure and schedule are being monitored
- The project remains viable
- The project gives value for money
- The project fits with strategy or programme.

User:
- User needs and expectations are being met or managed effectively
- An acceptable solution is being developed.

Specialist:
- Liaison is maintained between customer and supplier
- The needs of the specialist work of the project are recognised
- The scope of the project is not increasing unnoticed
- The required standards are being used correctly and are working.

Project Support

This role may be provided by a dedicated team to the project, or may be provided centrally supporting a number of projects, or may be provided by the Project Manager, depending on the size and nature of the project and the capabilities of the organisation.

Project Support covers:
- Configuration management
- Administration of project documentation and control, reviews, meetings and communications
- Providing expertise on support tools, estimating, planning and standards to the Project Manager.

Plans

In PRINCE2 the Project Plan and Stage Plans are mandatory plans. If the project uses a number of teams, there may also need to be Team Plans.

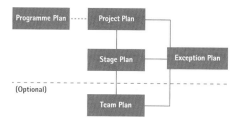

The Project Plan is a high-level document showing the key deliverables and major control points of the project. It summarises the resource requirements and costs and is used by the Project Board as a baseline against which to monitor actual costs and progress through the project.

A Stage Plan contains the level of detail needed for day-to-day control by the Project Manager. Each stage will have a Stage Plan which is produced as the current stage approaches completion.

Team Plans contain the more detailed activities of each Stage Plan and are usually prepared in parallel with the Stage Plan.

An Exception Plan may be produced at any point during a project. If the Project Manager forecasts in an Exception

Report that a stage may deviate beyond tolerance levels
set by the Project Board, the Project Board may respond
by requesting an Exception Plan to replace the remainder
of that plan. The same thing may happen if it is the Project
Plan or a Team Plan that is forecast to exceed its agreed
tolerances. The Exception Plan will replace the existing
plan showing the work and resources necessary to react
to the deviation.

All PRINCE2 plans contain the same information albeit
at different levels of detail:

- Graphical summary (such as Gantt chart)
- Resource and budget needs
- Description of the plan
- Prerequisites and assumptions
- External dependencies
- Risks
- Tolerances.

Controls
PRINCE2 controls help to ensure that the project is
producing the right products and to the right quality,
is being carried out according to schedule, and continues
to remain viable against its Business Case. The main
controls are the following:

Project initiation
Should the project be undertaken?

End stage assessment
Is the project still on course? Are risks under control?
Is the Business Case still viable? Should the next stage
be undertaken?

Highlight Reports
Regular reports from the Project Manager for the Project
Board.

Exception Reports
Early warning of any forecast deviation beyond tolerance
levels.

Project closure
Has the project delivered everything expected? What lessons
have been learned?

Stages
The division of the project into stages enables the Project
Board to control progress of the project. The Project Board
only commits to one stage at a time.

Tolerance
Tolerance is the allowable deviation from a plan without
needing to involve higher-level management. Tolerance
may be set against timescales, costs, scope, quality, risks
and benefits. If any plan is forecast to exceed the agreed
tolerance levels, the plan is in 'exception'.

Product Descriptions

Product Descriptions define the product to be delivered, the standards to be used or followed, the quality criteria to be applied to ensure the product is fit for purpose and the method to be used to check the product's quality.

Work Package

Work to be done by the project team is specified in a Work Package, which requires authorisation from the Project Manager before work can begin.

Project Issues

Project Issues may arise from any situation or source, including:

- User requirements change
- Legislation changes
- Organisation or business changes
- Suppliers being unable to deliver
- Resource availability changes
- Questions or concerns relating to the project.

In PRINCE2, all Project Issues are assessed to determine their impact on the project. All Project Issues raised are logged and any activities required to accommodate or resolve them are managed and documented.

Risk Log

All identified risks are logged and their analysis, countermeasures and status are regularly reviewed by the Project Manager and Project Board.

Management of risk

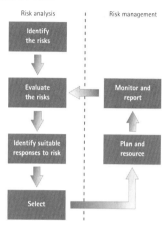

The task of risk management is to manage the project's exposure to risk by taking action to keep that exposure to an acceptable level in a cost-effective way.

Risk analysis involves the identification and evaluation of potential risks to any aspect of the project. Risk evaluation assesses the probability of the risk occurring and the impact on the project should the risk occur. Having identified the risks, possible actions to deal with the risks need to be considered and appropriate actions selected.

Actions to deal with risk include:

- *Prevention* – Terminate the risk by doing things differently and thus removing the risk, where it is feasible to do so. Countermeasures are put in place that either stop the threat or problem from occurring or prevent it having any impact on the project or business

- *Reduction* – Treat the risk; take action to control it in some way where the actions either reduce the likelihood of the risk developing or limit the impact on the project to acceptable levels
- *Transference* – This is a specialist form of risk reduction where the impact of the risk is passed to a third party via, for instance, an insurance policy or penalty clause
- *Acceptance* – Tolerate the risk, perhaps because nothing can be done at a reasonable cost to mitigate it, or the likelihood and impact of the risk occurring are at an acceptable level
- *Contingency* – These are actions planned and organised to come into force as and when the risk occurs.

Risk management involves planning and implementing the required resources to carry out the selected actions to deal with the risks. Once in place, the actions will require monitoring and reporting to ensure the risk management activities are having the desired effect.

The management of risk will be an ongoing activity throughout the project and will involve all members of the project organisation.

Quality in a project environment

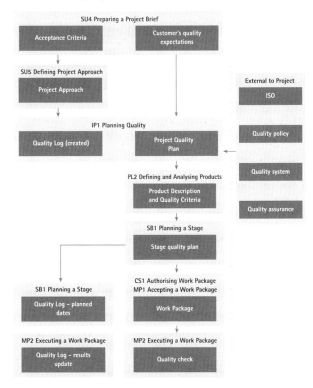

The quality standards and the responsibilities for ensuring quality is built into the project will be derived from a variety of sources, including the customer's quality expectations, requirements of ISO standards and existing quality management systems.

Planning for quality will involve agreement on:

- How each product will be tested against its quality criteria. Defined at the outset of the project
- When each product will be tested against its quality criteria. Defined in the relevant Stage or Team Plans
- By whom each product will be tested against its quality criteria. Defined in the relevant Stage or Team Plans.

Quality is achieved by a combination of actions:

- Defining quality criteria for each product in measurable terms
- Developing products according to the defined quality standards
- Checking for quality in all delivered products.

Configuration management

Configuration management is a major aspect of achieving quality control on a project. It provides the project with precise control over the project's assets. There are five basic functions within configuration management:

- *Planning* – Deciding the level of detail required
- *Identification* – Specifying all components of the final product
- *Control* – 'Freezing' products and then applying future changes under formal change control
- *Status accounting* – Recording and reporting all current and historical data about each product
- *Verification* – Reviewing and auditing to ensure the actual products match their records.

Change control

Throughout a project there will be various issues, changes and queries raised both from within the project and from stakeholders and other external interested parties. Change control provides a formal mechanism for ensuring all Project Issues are logged and considered, and appropriate action taken.

Consideration of Project Issues will involve assessing:
- The impact on the project's Business Case and projected benefits
- The impact on identified risks or the creation of new risks
- The impact on cost, time, quality or scope.

Project Issues that identify changes are either Requests for Change or Off-Specifications. Requests for Change identify a required change to a product; Off-Specifications identify that a product is likely to fail (or has failed) to achieve its requirements.

GLOSSARY OF PRINCE2 TERMS

Acceptance Criteria

A prioritised list of criteria that the final product(s) must meet before the customer will accept them; a measurable definition of what must be done for the final product to be acceptable to the customer. They should be defined as part of the Project Brief and agreed between customer and supplier no later than the project initiation stage. They should be documented in the Project Initiation Document.

Activity network

A flow diagram showing the activities of a plan and their interdependencies. The network shows each activity's duration, earliest start and finish times, latest start and finish times and float. Also known as 'planning network'. See also Critical path.

Baseline

A snapshot; a position or situation that is recorded. Although the position may be updated later, the baseline remains unchanged and available as a reminder of the original state and as a comparison against the current position. Products that have passed their quality checks and are approved are baselined products. Anything 'baselined' should be under version control in configuration management and 'frozen', i.e. no changes to that version are allowed.

Benefits
The positive outcomes, quantified or unquantified, that a project is being undertaken to deliver and that justify the investment.

Benefits realisation
The practice of ensuring that the outcome of a project produces the projected benefits claimed in the Business Case.

Business Case
Information that describes the justification for setting up and continuing a PRINCE2 project. It provides the reasons (and answers the question: 'Why?') for the project. An outline Business Case should be in the Project Mandate. Its existence is checked as part of the Project Brief, and a revised, fuller version appears in the Project Initiation Document. It is updated at key points, such as end stage assessments, throughout the project.

Change authority
A group to which the Project Board may delegate responsibility for the consideration of Requests for Change. The change authority is given a budget and can approve changes within that budget.

Change budget
The money allocated to the change authority to be spent on authorised Requests for Change.

Change control
The procedure to ensure that the processing of all Project Issues is controlled, including submission, analysis and decision making.

Checkpoint
A team-level, time-driven review of progress, usually involving a meeting.

Checkpoint Report
A progress report of the information gathered at a checkpoint meeting which is given by a team to the Project Manager and provides reporting data as defined in the Work Package.

Communication Plan
Part of the Project Initiation Document describing how the project's stakeholders and interested parties will be kept informed during the project.

Concession
An Off-Specification that is accepted by the Project Board without corrective action.

Configuration audit
A comparison of the latest version number and status of all products shown in the configuration library records against the information held by the product authors.

Configuration control
Configuration control is concerned with physically controlling receipt and issue of products, keeping track

of product status, protecting finished products and
controlling any changes to them.

Configuration management
A discipline, normally supported by software tools, that
gives management precise control over its assets (for
example, the products of a project), covering planning,
identification, control, status accounting and verification
of the products.

Contingency budget
The amount of money required to implement a contingency
plan. If the Project Board approves a contingency plan,
it would normally set aside a contingency budget, which
would only be called upon if the contingency plan had
to be implemented when the associated risk occurs.
See also Contingency plan.

Contingency plan
A plan that provides details of the measures to be taken if
a defined risk should occur. The plan is only implemented
if the risk occurs. A contingency plan is prepared where
other actions (risk prevention, reduction or transfer) are
not possible, too expensive or the current view is that the
cost of the risk occurring does not sufficiently outweigh
the cost of taking avoiding action – but the risk cannot be
simply accepted. The Project Board can see that, should
the risk occur, there is a plan of action to counter it. If the
Project Board agrees that this is the best form of action,
it would put aside a contingency budget, the cost of the
contingency plan, only to be used if the risk occurs.

Critical path

This is the line connecting the start of an activity network with the final activity in that network through those activities with zero float, i.e. those activities where any delay will delay the time of the entire end date of the plan. There may be more than one such path. The sum of the activity durations on the critical path will determine the end date of the plan.

Customer

The person or group who commissioned the work and will benefit from the end results.

Customer's quality expectations

A statement from the customer about the quality expected from the final product. This should be obtained during the start-up of a project in *Preparing a Project Brief* (SU4) as an important feed into *Planning Quality* (IP1), where it is matched against the Project Approach and the standards that will need to be applied in order to achieve that quality.

Daily Log

A record of jobs to do or to check that others have done, commitments from the author or others, important events, decisions or discussions. A Daily Log should be kept by the Project Manager and any Team Managers.

Deliverable

An item that the project has to create as part of the requirements. It may be part of the final outcome or an intermediate element on which one or more subsequent deliverables are dependent. According to the type of project, another name for a deliverable is 'product'.

Earned value analysis

Earned value analysis is a method for measuring project performance. It indicates how much of the budget should have been spent in view of the amount of work done so far and the task, assignment or resources.

End Project Report

A report given by the Project Manager to the Project Board that confirms the handover of all products and provides an updated Business Case and an assessment of how well the project has done against its Project Initiation Document.

End stage assessment

The review by the Project Board and Project Manager of the End Stage Report to decide whether to approve the next Stage Plan (unless the last stage has now been completed). According to the size and criticality of the project, the review may be formal or informal. The approval to proceed should be documented as an important management product.

End Stage Report

A report given by the Project Manager to the Project Board at the end of each management stage of the project. This provides information about the project performance during the stage and the project status at stage end.

Exception

A situation where it can be forecast that there will be a deviation beyond the tolerance levels agreed between the Project Manager and the Project Board (or between the Project Board and corporate or programme management, or between a Team Manager and the Project Manager).

Exception assessment

This is a meeting of the Project Board to approve (or reject) an Exception Plan.

Exception Plan

This is a plan that often follows an Exception Report. For a Team Plan exception, it covers the period from the present to the end of the Work Package; for a Stage Plan exception, it covers the period from the present to the end of the current stage. If the exception were at a project level, the Project Plan would be replaced.

Exception Report

Description of the exception situation, its impact, options, recommendation and impact of the recommendation to the Project Board. This report is prepared by the relevant manager to inform the next higher level of management of the situation.

Executive

The single individual with overall responsibility for ensuring that a project meets its objectives and delivers the projected benefits. This individual should ensure that the project or programme maintains its business focus, that it has clear authority and that the work, including risks, is actively managed. The Executive is the chairperson of the Project Board, representing the customer, and is the owner of the Business Case.

Feasibility study
A feasibility study is an early study of a problem to assess if a solution is feasible. The study will normally scope the problem, identify and explore a number of solutions, and make a recommendation on what action to take. Part of the work in developing options is to calculate an outline Business Case for each as one aspect of comparison.

Follow-on Action Recommendations
A report that can be used as input to the process of creating a Business Case/Project Mandate for any follow-on PRINCE2 project and for recording any follow-on instructions covering incomplete products or outstanding Project Issues.

Gantt chart
This is a diagram of a plan's activities against a time background, showing start and end times and resources required.

Gate review
A generic term, rather than a PRINCE2 term, meaning a point at the end of a stage or phase where a decision is made whether to continue with the project. In PRINCE2 this would equate to an end stage assessment.

Highlight Report
Time-driven report from the Project Manager to the Project Board on stage progress.

Issue Log
Contains all Project Issues including Requests for Change raised during the project. Project Issues are each allocated a unique number and are filed in the Issue Log under the appropriate status. See also Project Issue.

Lessons Learned Log
An informal collection of good and bad lessons learned about the management and specialist processes and products as the project progresses. At the end of the project, it is formalised and structured into a Lessons Learned Report. See also Lessons Learned Report.

Lessons Learned Report
A report that describes the lessons learned in undertaking the project and includes statistics from the quality control of the project's management products. It is approved by the Project Board and then held centrally for the benefit of future projects.

Off-Specification
Something that should be provided by the project, but currently is not (or is forecast not to be) provided. This might be a missing product or a product not meeting its specifications. It is one type of Project Issue.

Operational and maintenance acceptance
Acceptance by the person/group who will support the product during its useful life that it is accepted into the operational environment. The format of the acceptance will depend on the product itself – it could be in the form of an acceptance letter signed by the appropriate authority, or a more complex report detailing the operational and maintenance arrangements that have been put in place.

Outcome
The term used to describe the totality of what the project is set up to deliver, consisting of all the specialist products. For example, this could be an installed computer system with trained staff to use it, backed up by new working practices and documentation, a refurbished and equipped building with all the staff moved in and working, or it could be a new product launched with a recruited and trained sales and support team in place.

Peer review
Specific reviews of a project or any of its products where personnel from within the organisation and/or from other organisations carry out an independent assessment of the project. Peer reviews can be done at any point within a project but are often used at stage-end points.

Phase
A part, section or segment of a project, similar in meaning to a PRINCE2 stage. The key meaning of stage in PRINCE2 terms is the use of management stages, i.e. sections of the project to which the Project Board commits one at a time.

A phase might be more connected to a time slice, change of skills required or change of emphasis.

Post-implementation review
See Post-project review.

Post-project review
One or more reviews held after project closure to determine if the expected benefits have been obtained. Also known as post-implementation review.

PRINCE2
A method that supports some selected aspects of project management. The acronym stands for **PR**ojects **IN** **C**ontrolled **E**nvironments.

PRINCE2 project
A project whose product(s) can be defined at its start sufficiently precisely so as to be measurable against predefined metrics and that is managed according to the PRINCE2 method.

Process
That which must be done to bring about a particular result in terms of information to be gathered, decisions to be made and results to be achieved.

Producer
This role represents the creator(s) of a product that is the subject of a quality review. Typically, it will be filled by the person who has produced the product or who has led the team responsible.

Product

Any input to or output from a project. PRINCE2 distinguishes between management products (which are produced as part of the management or quality processes of the project) and specialist products (which are those products that make up the final deliverable). A product may itself be a collection of other products.

Product-based planning

A four-step technique leading to a comprehensive plan based on creation and delivery of required outputs. The technique considers prerequisite products, quality requirements and the dependencies between products.

Product Breakdown Structure

A hierarchy of all the products to be produced during a plan.

Product Checklist

A list of the major products of a plan, plus key dates in their delivery.

Product Description

A description of a product's purpose, composition, derivation and quality criteria. It is produced at planning time, as soon as possible after the need for the product is identified.

Product Flow Diagram

A diagram showing the sequence of production and interdependencies of the products listed in a Product Breakdown Structure.

Product life span

This term is used in this manual to define the total life of a product from the time of the initial idea for the product until it is removed from service. It is likely that there will be many projects affecting the product during its life, such as a feasibility study and development, enhancement or correction projects.

Product Status Account

A report on the status of products. The required products can be specified by identifier or the part of the project in which they were developed.

Programme

A portfolio of projects selected, planned and managed in a co-ordinated way.

Project

A temporary organisation that is created for the purpose of delivering one or more business products according to a specified Business Case.

Project Approach

A description of the way in which the work of the project is to be approached. For example: Are we building a product from scratch or buying in a product that already exists? Are the technology and products that we can use constrained by decisions taken at programme level?

Project Assurance

The Project Board's responsibilities to assure itself that the project is being conducted correctly.

Project Brief
A description of what the project is to do; a refined and extended version of the Project Mandate, which the Project Board approves and which is input to project initiation.

Project closure notification
Advice from the Project Board to inform all stakeholders and the host location that the project resources can be disbanded and support services, such as space, equipment and access, demobilised. It should indicate a closure date for costs to be charged to the project.

Project closure recommendation
A recommendation prepared by the Project Manager for the Project Board to send as a project closure notification when the board is satisfied that the project can be closed.

Project Initiation Document (PID)
A logical document that brings together the key information needed to start the project on a sound basis and to convey that information to all concerned with the project.

Project Issue
A term used to cover any concern, query, Request for Change, suggestion or Off-Specification raised during the project. They can be about anything to do with the project.

Project life cycle
This term is used in this manual to define the period from the start-up of a project to the handover of the finished product to those who will operate and maintain it.

Project management

The planning, monitoring and control of all aspects of a project and the motivation of all those involved in it to achieve the project objectives on time and to the specified cost, quality and performance.

Project management team

Covers the entire management structure of Project Board, Project Manager, plus any Team Manager, Project Assurance and Project Support roles.

Project Manager

The person given the authority and responsibility to manage the project on a day-to-day basis to deliver the required products within the constraints agreed with the Project Board.

Project Mandate

Information created externally to the project that forms the terms of reference and is used to start up the PRINCE2 project.

Project Plan

A high-level plan showing the major products of the project, when they will be delivered and at what cost. An initial Project Plan is presented as part of the Project Initiation Document. This is revised as information on actual progress appears. It is a major control document for the Project Board to measure actual progress against expectations.

Project Quality Plan

A plan defining the key quality criteria, quality control and audit processes to be applied to project management and specialist work in the PRINCE2 project. It will be part of the text in the Project Initiation Document.

Project records

A collection of all approved management and specialist products and other material, which is necessary to provide an auditable record of the project. Note: This does not include working files.

Project start-up notification

Advice to the host location that the project is about to start and requesting any required Project Support services.

Project Support

An administrative role in the project management team. Project Support can be in the form of advice and help with project management tools, guidance, administrative services such as filing, and the collection of actual data. The provision of any Project Support on a formal basis is optional. Tasks either need to be done by the Project Manager or delegated to a separate body and this will be driven by the needs of the individual project and Project Manager.

One support function that must be considered is that of configuration management. Depending on the project size and environment, there may be a need to formalise this and it quickly becomes a task with which the Project Manager cannot cope without support.

Project Support Office
A group set up to provide certain administrative services to the Project Manager. Often the group provides its services to many projects in parallel.

Proximity (of risk)
Reflects the timing of the risk, i.e. is the threat (or opportunity) stronger at a particular time, does it disappear some time in the future, or does the probability or impact change over time?

Quality
The totality of features and characteristics of a product or service that bear on its ability to satisfy stated needs. Also defined as 'fitness for purpose' or 'conforms to requirements'.

Quality Log
Contains all planned and completed quality activities. The Quality Log is used by the Project Manager and Project Assurance as part of reviewing progress.

Quality management system
The complete set of quality standards, procedures and responsibilities for a site or organisation.

Quality review
A quality review is a quality checking technique with a specific structure, defined roles and procedure designed to ensure a product's completeness and adherence to standards. The participants are drawn from those with an interest in the product and those with the necessary skills to review its correctness. An example of the checks made

by a quality review is: 'Does the document match the quality criteria in the Product Description?'

Quality system
See Quality management system.

Request for Change
A means of proposing a modification to the current specification of a product. It is one type of Project Issue.

Requirements
A description of the user's needs. See also Specification.

Reviewer
A person asked to review a product that is the subject of a quality review.

Risk
Risk can be defined as uncertainty of outcome, whether positive opportunity or negative threat. Every project has risks associated with it. Project management has the task of identifying risks that apply and taking appropriate steps to take advantage of opportunities that may arise and avoid, reduce or react to threats.

Risk Log
Contains all information about the risks, their analysis, countermeasures and status. Also known as Risk Register.

Risk profile
A graphical representation of information normally found in the Risk Log.

Risk register
See Risk Log.

Risk tolerance line
The risk tolerance line is one drawn between risks that can
be accepted or for which suitable actions have been planned,
and risks that that are considered sufficiently serious to
require referral to the next higher level of project authority.

Senior responsible owner
This is not a PRINCE2 term, but is used in many
organisations. Its equivalent in PRINCE2 terms would
be the 'Executive' role. See also Executive.

Senior Supplier
The Project Board role that provides knowledge and
experience of the main discipline(s) involved in the
production of the project's deliverable(s). Represents
the supplier interests within the project and provides
supplier resources.

Senior User
The Project Board role accountable for ensuring that user
needs are specified correctly and that the solution meets
those needs.

Specification
A detailed statement of what the user wants in terms of
products, what these should look like, what they should do
and with what they should interface.

Sponsor

Not a specific PRINCE2 role but often used to mean the major driving force of a project. May be the equivalent of Executive or corporate/programme management.

Stage

A stage is the section of the project that the Project Manager is managing on behalf of the Project Board at any one time, at the end of which the Project Board wishes to review progress to date, the state of the Project Plan, Business Case and risks, and the next Stage Plan in order to decide whether to continue with the project.

Stakeholders

Parties with an interest in the execution and outcome of a project. They would include business streams affected by or dependent on the outcome.

Supplier

The group or groups responsible for the supply of the project's specialist products.

Team Manager

A role that may be employed by the Project Manager or Senior Supplier to manage the work of project team members.

Tolerance

The permissible deviation above and below a plan's estimate of time and cost without escalating the deviation to the next level of management. Separate tolerance figures should be given for time and cost. There may also be tolerance levels for quality, scope, benefit and risk. Tolerance is applied at project, stage and team levels.

User(s)

The person or group who will use the final deliverable(s) of the project.

Work Package

The set of information relevant to the creation of one or more products. It will contain a description of the work, the Product Description(s), details of any constraints on production such as time and cost, interfaces, and confirmation of the agreement between the Project Manager and the person or Team Manager who is to implement the Work Package that the work can be done within the constraints.